EPSO

10
TOWN AND
COUNTRY
RAMBLES

CHRIS HOWKINS &
MARGARET EGGLETON

PUBLISHED BY
CHRIS HOWKINS

PUBLISHED BY

Chris Howkins, 70 Grange Road,
New Haw, Addlestone, Surrey
KT15 3RH.

PRINTED BY

Ian Allan Printing, Coombelands
House, Coombelands Lane,
Addlestone, Surrey KT15 1HY.

Detail of
Epsom
Clocktower

TEXT AND ILLUSTRATIONS: CHRIS HOWKINS AND
                          MARGARET EGGLETON

COPYRIGHT: CHRIS HOWKINS © 1993

ISBN 0 9319348 3 X

CONTENTS

INTRODUCTION

When thin sunshine parts the winter mist to show a
string of race horses wheezing across the Downs in
clouds of white breath then you know you have found a
very singular corner of Surrey. There is so much to
see and enjoy around Epsom and this book, like the
others in the series, sets out to introduce some of
that variety and interest. The rambles are kept short
to allow for this but some can be linked together for
longer ventures.

For this edition I am very grateful to local artist
Margaret Eggleton for the sketches and drawings of
architectural subjects. Her differing styles add a
welcome variety. Although well known for teaching art
to adults and children, and for having her work
exhibited widely, this is the first time her drawings
have been published in book form. Additionally, Mrs.
Eggleton has given time and trouble to choosing and
preparing some of the rambles.

Ewell Prison

4

M.E.
Nonsuch

The rest of the illustrations and production is mine.
All the routes were checked in the winter of 1992-3
but changes will be inevitable. Notification of these
would be welcome at the publisher's address ready for
revising any future edition.

The maps, simplified and not to scale, are intended to
give only a visual indication of the route. Follow the
directions in the text not the map. Please note that the
inclusion of a route is not a guarantee that it is a
public right of way. The landowners may well make changes
to public access.

The countryside is particularly beautiful in winter but
then parts of the Epsom area go under glorious mud. As
mud is not everyone's idea of the glorious rambles at
Ashtead, Ewell and Nonsuch were sought out for their
surfaced paths. Parts of Headley Heath are on clean sand
and the routes over chalk dry out quickly. For those who
enjoy a good muddy squelch try Ashtead Common and Epsom
Ponds. The latter is a "wander at will" site for those
who dislike following directions all the time.

Enjoy the Epsom district. It will no doubt surprise many
that, despite being on the edge of suburbia, it is so
rural.   c.H.

LOCATION MAP OF THE RAMBLES

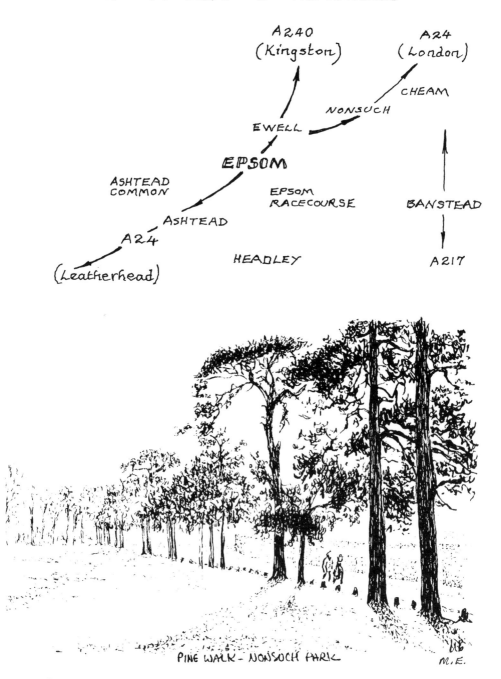

A240
(Kingston)

A24
(London)

CHEAM

NONSUCH

EWELL

EPSOM

ASHTEAD
COMMON

EPSOM
RACECOURSE

BANSTEAD

ASHTEAD

A24

HEADLEY

A217

(Leatherhead)

PINE WALK - NONSUCH PARK

M.E.

EPSOM TOWN : Georgian Architecture etc.

DISTANCE: 2·3 miles or 4·3 miles if extended to the Downs. Can be linked to Racecourse Ramble and Ashtead.

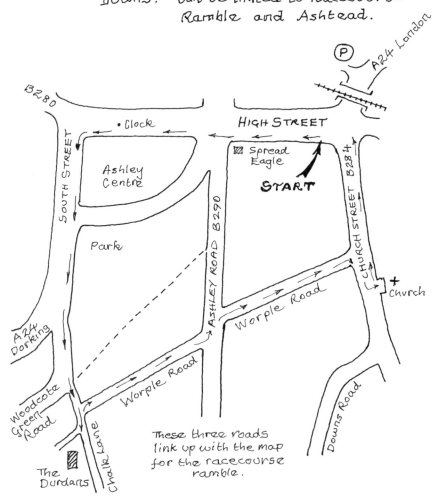

WHEELS: Easy going on the pavements for both push-chairs and wheelchairs, kerbs and steps into church excepted, but it is a long slog up to the Downs for wheelchairs if the extension is being considered, or entry to the town from that direction.

FAIR WARNING ! Epsom High Street is a major bottleneck on the A24, controlled by several sets of traffic lights, so expect delays. Car parking can be difficult and the side streets are well decorated with yellow lines. For the energetic, consider parking at the race course and walking down into the town. The south of this map joins the north of the racecourse map.

EPSOM IS NOTED for its late Stuart, Queen Anne and Georgian architecture. Most lies to the south in the Woodcote district through which this ramble passes but there is only room here to draw attention to a few of the buildings. More will be found en route.

Epsom Clock Tower

START at the east end of the High Street and begin walking westwards along it, preferably on the south side. Look across to the very long block on the north side, built in classical style earlier this century. It creates great unity over the small shop units below but boredom has been prevented by the careful changes in vertical detailing all the way along.

CROSS central cross roads to continue along High Street. Note on the corner, the Spread Eagle building - one of the few noticeably old buildings to survive along here. Ahead, the Clock Tower (1847-8) dominates as it was meant to; a landscape feature unrivalled in Surrey and one of the most imposing public lavatories in the whole country. Around it a street market is held still, to add character to this busy centre.

TURN LEFT out of the end of the High Street into South Street where the first part has some of the older buildings; nothing very grand. On the left the flowers and seats of the public park invite a detour. Epsom has a good collection of mature trees, some of which are of the scarcer species.

8

BEAR LEFT up Woodcote Green Road and this rather tame
stretch is soon relieved by a delightful corner of old
buildings where Chalk Lane makes a little junction on
the left, (NO ENTRY to cars so don't try cheating!)
This group can be very photogenic in the right light and
in any case is worth viewing from several angles. The
footway on the left returns to town centre.

TURN LEFT through the group to go up Chalk Lane.
Another good grouping lies ahead, after the pub on the
right. Best is Maidstone House, from the mid-Georgian
period, with very nice detailing from its gates up to
its pineapple finials to the parapet. Doorcase and the
Venetian windows work up a good front elevation.
The Chalk Lane Hotel opposite is quite a contrast but
is early 18th century too. All this grouping has grown
up beyond the great house in the park - Durdans - beyond.
It is about the only great Epsom house to survive. To
get a glimpse of one of its elevations continue up Chalk
Lane a little way. Notice the great gates which are
contemporary and fine examples of the craft.

THE DURDANS
Built 1764-8
by W.Newton.

Extended in
19th century.

RETURN a little way down Chalk
Lane. (To continue up the lane
is to reach the alternative
car parking site at the
race course).

TURN RIGHT into Worple
Road and so to Ashley
Road. Cross it and
continue along
Worple Road to
Church Street.

High Street, Epsom

TURN RIGHT to walk up Church Street to the church.
Note first, on the right hand corner, The Cedars, which is of
particular architectural importance, from the late 17th/
early 18th century, with its arms over the door. Then, on the
right, No.18 of the same period. Opposite is Richmond House,
good early 19th century, followed by Beechwood. Then over on
the right an oblique view of the impressive front of Park
Place House. On the left, Stone House, 18th century, and so
around the corner into the little church square.

The church has an interesting history and is worth a
visit. The west front gives no indication of the
beautiful lit interior with work ranging from the
late medieval period to the present century when work
began on upgrading the building to cathedral status.
See displays inside for the full details.

RETURN down Church Street to the Start.
After the Worple Road junction note on the right, the
United Reformed Church - once so modern and now looking
dull. On the left notice the unusually grand Royal Arms
on the front of the Police Station. The striking
terracotta building ahead (Education Centre) bears the
date 1895 - one of the better Victorian frontages.
Look back to see how the recent Kirkgate building has
been designed to fit its corner site so well.

Epsom Town Hall

EPSOM RACECOURSE : Chalk Downland

DISTANCE : 3 miles approx
For extensions see below

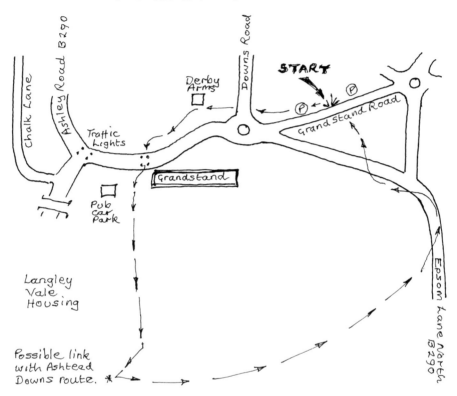

EXTENDING THE RAMBLE

This ramble can be joined on to that for Epsom Town
Centre; the top of this map joins the bottom of the
other. Chalk Lane is the most pleasant linking route.

This ramble can also be joined to the Ashtead Downs
ramble — see end of this section for link directions.

WHEELS : Not recommended — rough and steep.

AVOID the area on days when there are race meetings.
This ramble not possible on those days.

This is a hilly chalkland ramble over
the Downs where "the public have rights
of air and exercise on foot". There
is always a sense of open airy space
and, in summer, the special wild
flowers of the chalk. It does not
get too muddy even in a wet winter.

young
Robin

START in lay-by car park on the
crest of the Downs (Grand Stand Road).
The features of the panoramic view view over London
can be identified from the viewing point mid-length of
the car park. If wind has cleared the London smog the
view stretches to North London (Highgate Church) but
unexpectedly St.Paul's Cathedral is even further away
at 24.5 mls.

TURN TO THE LEFT and follow the grassy edge round
to the Derby Arms, bearing on its front elevation the
equestrian portrait of the first Derby winner - Diomed.

CONTINUE PAST THE PUB to the pedestrian crossing
and use it. The grandstand has been recently restored,
to good effect. Parts go back to the early years of
this century. Its predecessor had an upper flat wherein
lived Mrs Beeton of Household Management fame.

BEAR RIGHT and follow the surfaced path to the
designated crossing point of the racecourse and then
proceed ahead through the car park of the Rubbing House

Pub. Head for the map and information
board on the edge of the grassland
in front of you. Good idea to check
the regulations on it! Follow the
narrow but clear footpath from the
right of the board, heading directly
away towards the crest of the Downs.
The air is often rich with the song
of Skylarks; the birds illustrated
are a parent and young Robin found
in the car park. You need to keep
going in roughly the same direction,
so don't worry about side paths and
alternative ways.

14

CROSS surfaced road and then the race track (Derby
starting point on the right) on to a dirt track and
follow it. Ramblers should remember this
is a working landscape so be prepared
for horses and control children
and dogs accordingly.

Derby
Arms.

CROSS
another of
the training tracks
at the designated spot
and continue downhill towards the
trees. KEEP GOING through the woods and up the other
side. When the trees stop still continue ahead, over
the brow and down through the pastures.

There is a rich variety of wildlife through here, with
the mixture of grassland and woods, sun and shade.

TURN LEFT at the bottom (link point with the Ashtead Downs ramble - see following section).

Yellow hammers

FOLLOW
this route
round in an
anti-clockwise
direction, to
reach the road
(Epsom Lane North)
beside the racecourse.
Continue bearing left,
wisest to cross onto the pavement
for a short stretch before crossing back onto the more
enjoyable grass. This bend round is the Tattenham
Corner made famous on racing commentaries and where
the suffragette, Emily Davison, brought down the King's
horse in the 1913 Derby.

The starting point lies ahead to the right of the grand
stand, so depart from the trackside to cross the roads
back to the car park.

MAP FOR LINKING THE EPSOM RACECOURSE ROUTE TO THE ASHTEAD DOWNS ROUTE.

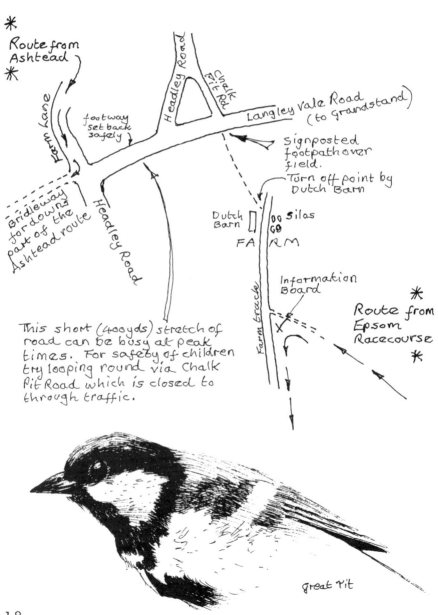

* Route from Ashtead *

Headley Road

Chalk Pit Rd

Langley Vale Road (to grandstand)

footway set back safely

Farm Lane

Bridleway for downs part of the Ashtead route

Headley Road

Signposted footpath over field.

Turn off point by Dutch Barn

Dutch Barn

oo Silos oo

FA RM

Information Board

Farm track

* Route from Epsom Racecourse *

This short (400 yds) stretch of road can be busy at peak times. For safety of children try looping round via Chalk Pit Road which is closed to through traffic.

great tit

18

ASHTEAD AND THE DOWNS : Village
Gardens and Lanes

DISTANCE : 3 miles approx
Can be linked with Epsom Racecourse route.

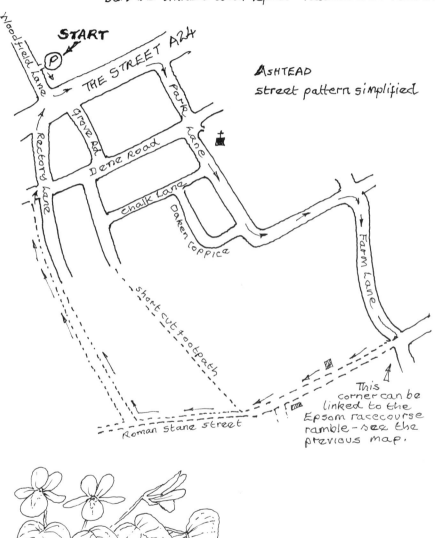

START

Woodfield Lane

THE STREET A24

Grove Rd.

Dene Road

Chalk Lane

Rectory Lane

Park Lane

Oaken Coppice

Short cut footpath

Farm Lane

Roman Stane Street

ASHTEAD
street pattern simplified

This corner can be linked to the Epsom racecourse ramble - see the previous map.

The Street, Ashtead

EXTENDING THE RAMBLE : The car park is on the same Woodfield Lane that leads to the start of the ramble on Ashtead Common so these could easily be added together.

The previous map shows how to link the upper part of this ramble to that over Epsom Racecourse.

In this ramble there is a short optional visit to the village pond, to feed the ducks and gulls in winter if you have young children with you.

This ramble has been chosen for those who like a clean,
comfortable route in winter, when so much of the local
countryside becomes rather muddy. With so many trees
the route is recommended for spring greens and autumn
russets and gold; for summer shade and flowers. The
village goes back to Saxon times, when there was an
important burial ground here, and before that, to when
the Romans lived and worked in this countryside. For
the easiest ramble stay in the grid of lanes to the
south east side of The Street; otherwise follow the
directions up on to the top of the Downs.

WHEELS : The lower part of the route is suitable. The
upper part is not suitable for wheelchairs but is
passable for pushchairs wil one short stretch of
dragging.

THE BREWERY INN

Ashtead Village . Surrey

PARKING: Turn off the A24 in the middle of The Street
into Woodfield Lane and there is a car park on the right.
Turn right out of it for the "quick option" on the next
page or turn left to start the main ramble.

QUICK OPTION

For just a few minutes fresh air, perhaps in coldest
winter, try a visit to the village pond. Turn right out
of the car park and the pond is on the left at the end
of the lane. On the way look out for two old cottages
from the 17th/18th centuries.

The pond is always a pleasant spot to pause, perhaps on
the way to the Ashtead Common Ramble, but in winter
when it ices over there are many ducks, gulls etc. all
keen to take food. This is therefore a good spot to
introduce young children to our birds.

MAIN RAMBLE

TURN LEFT out of the car park and up Woodfield Lane.
TURN LEFT along The Street. This is not one of the
very old Surrey streets as the main road to Epsom used
to pass through at a higher level, by the church. All
the same, this one loops and twists attractively as it
follows the contours of the land and it has an open
airy feel with plenty of sky overhead. Consequently
there are only a few old buildings along here, such as
Nos 44/46 from the 17th century.

Cross over to the right hand pavement and near the end seek a Victorian-looking house which bears a dedication stone informing us that this was built as an almshouse in 1843 although the original foundation was back in 1736. This 'hospital' for six poor widows of the parish was due to Lady Diana Fielding and just for once we can 'meet' the lady for there is a beautiful marble portrait of her in the church.

TURN RIGHT up Park Lane, where the trees and gardens are attractive immediately, even if most of the housing is 20th century.

AT THE CROSSROADS cross over to enter the church approach. This is the old heart of Ashtead, a pre-Christian site with earthworks believed to date from the Roman period. The yew tree in the churchyard is also claimed to be pre-Christian.

ST GILES CHURCH has a good 16th century tower in the Thames Valley style but the rest of the church was rebuilt in 1862. The roof timbering has been described as "preposterous" by Ian Nairn and indeed there is a lot of fussy detailing but the main beams are terrific with Victorian gusto.

St. Giles, Ashtead

The church is worth a visit for it retains the late
medieval font and the memorial brasses including that
to John Browne, Serjeant of the Woodyard for Elizabeth
I. The stained glass in the east window contains a 16th
century Crucifixion scene from Herck near Maastricht.
Two monuments are of note, one for being so bad and
the other for being so good. The former is to Henry

24

Newdigate and is believed to be by Grinling Gibbons, in which case it should be a masterpiece but it isn't. The other is to Diana Fielding, aforementioned, and rises to the quality of Rysbrack.

RETURN TO THE ROAD AND TURN LEFT to continue up Park Lane. These lanes are a delight in spring when the leaves are coming out. Look for Chalk Lane on the right because this is the best option to take, to ramble through to Rectory Lane at the end, for anyone not wishing to go on up to the Downs. Otherwise, follow Park Lane round to the left and on to the end.

TURN RIGHT up Farm Lane to climb uphill to the next junction. Again, the trees in spring and autumn can give a lot of pleasure. There is more traffic on this road so take care; it isn't very far.

TURN RIGHT at the junction on to a surfaced track. Alternatively, anyone planning to join this ramble to that for Epsom Racecourse should turn left as per the map printed before this section. From this junction you walk into the working landscape of the racing stables so be prepared for horses and give them precedence. No visit to Epsom is complete without a sighting of the race horses and two stables are coming up now, one on the right and then one on the left (no public access of course). After the second stables the track turns left but keep to the right side to continue walking ahead up a bridleway.

CONTINUE AHEAD off the surfaced track, up the rutted bridleway and so out into the fields at the top. Being on chalk this does not get too muddy in winter.

Hardy cyclamen in a garden.

According to the Ordnance Survey map this route across the fields is the route of Stane Street, the Roman road from the South Coast to London. A signposted footpath off to the right can be taken to return to Ashtead. Otherwise continue ahead towards the woods and walk in under the stately Beech trees with their slim noble trunks – their timber is still of great economic importance in Britain. The Beech is still the tree most associated with the chalk Downs but this was not always so; originally the hills were clothed over in Oak woods but as these were felled for timber to provide an everyday resource so the Beech sprang up in its place, from the 13th century onwards. It was still happening in the 17th century when it was described by John Evelyn the diarist, with Surrey estates near Dorking.

TURN RIGHT on entering this stand (before the pylon) to follow the trackway downhill. (Ramblers can continue ahead along Stane Street but will need to return the same way.) Follow the track right down to the road. Note the ancient boundary bank and ditches along the right side.

TURN RIGHT to step into Rectory Lane and then left to follow the lane down to The Street where it emerges nearly opposite the end of Woodfield Lane and the car park. During this short descent there are more old cottages to look out for as you re-enter the older part of present day Ashtead.

Oak spangle galls.

26

EPSOM COMMON : Woodland and Grassland.
Detour to the Well.

DISTANCE : 2 miles with options to extend

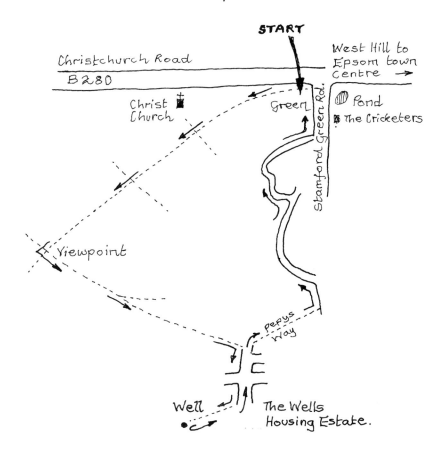

THIS is a pleasant easy-going ramble but be
prepared for the long grass to be wet after rain.

WHEELS: It is possible for push-chairs but
wheelchairs will need energy!

START : Continue eastwards out of
the High Street along West Hill
until there is a green on the
left at the bottom of a
dip. There is a pond on
the corner and the
Cricketers pub along
on the left. Street
parking for motorists.

STAMFORD GREEN
CRICKET CLUB

This is one of Epsom's
surprises. The urban
centre seems miles away,
replaced by a village-
style scene with pub
and pond with ducks, a grassy green and a backing of
trees. FOLLOW along the bottom of the green but
skirt up round to the left, leaving the road behind,
to follow the widest path into the trees. Lesser paths
join up with it.

CONTINUE uphill through the trees. Enjoy the apple
blossom in spring or the colour of the fruit in the
autumn but don't bother eating one. These are crab
apples, degenerate apples that sprang from the pips
in cores thrown away by walkers years ago.

The other shrubby trees, with black berries in autumn,
are Alder Buckthorns, used formerly for many things
from dyes to medicines and even gunpowder charcoal
(used in the Falklands War). The berries have a toxic
effect so teach children to recognise and respect them.

CROSS the surfaced path and CROSS another path,
always continuing uphill. The scrub woodland gives way
to open grassland, although being invaded rapidly by
scrub. Note the odd Gorse bush and patch of Heather
showing that this was once open heathland - one of the
most valuable habitats in Surrey but now being overgrown and lost, like this one.

28

TURN LEFT at the junction in the rides at the crest of the rise. There is a good long-distance view from here. The nearby shrubs are best enjoyed in autumn when the Dogwoods have white berries and the Spindles have fruits of orange and crimson. Both shrubs have been of service to man in the past but don't eat the berries of either of them.

TURN LEFT on to the surfaced track. Gardens are being approached on this side of the common and so there is a greater variety of birds to look out for.

BEAR RIGHT at the fork and continue to the smoother surfaced road. Here you need to TURN LEFT BUT to visit the well TURN RIGHT and head for the houses and shops (refreshments available). WALK STRAIGHT AHEAD all the way down Spa Drive to the very end.

TURN LEFT down Wickens Way which is only a footpath and at the end the well is on your left, with modern brick surround, iron overmantle and inscription. It is not very exciting but there it is!

RETRACE your steps to the shops and so back on to the common to FOLLOW Pepys Way through the woods and out to the road. FOLLOW that ahead, going downhill, past the turn-of-the-century villas that crept on to the common as it went out of use, and so to the green and the starting point.

View of Christchurch though the trees on Epsom Common

EPSOM COMMON PONDS : Waterside Wildlife

DISTANCE : 1½ miles with options to extend.

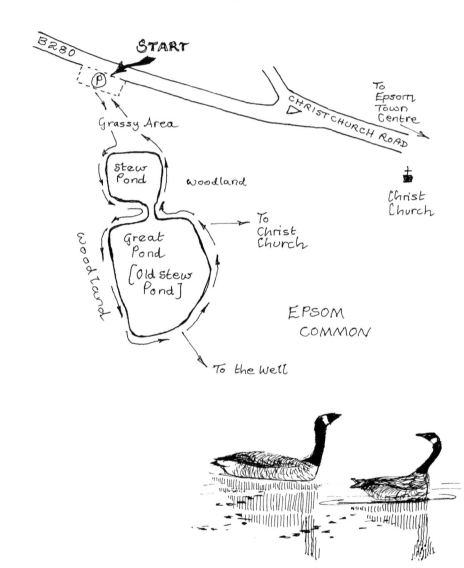

WHEELS: Unsuitable except around the
car park/grassy area.

Water always proves attractive and these two ponds are no exception, especially since local volunteers took the site in hand for restoration work. The large pond in particular had become very overgrown. Both are man-made ponds, made watertight with local clay off the common and filled with spring water. Now it is once again a pleasant spot for wildlife, anglers and visitors. This is not a place to hurry so the route described is simply round the ponds but there is scope for more...

to extend the ramble there are the many acres of Epsom Common all around to explore at will, or else try a link up with the Epsom Common ramble in this book.

LOCATION: West of Epsom on the B280 as per the Epsom Common ramble but instead of turning into Stamford Green Road continue ahead, bearing left at the junction. Look for the car park on the left hand side.

Canada Geese preening.

PARKING : car park provided

RAMBLE : This is an excellent place to WANDER AT WILL for those who do not wish to be bossed around by directions.

For guidance - cross the grassy area by the first pond and then wander round the waterside of both ponds.

MUD : Plenty in winter and after wet weather.

Top ~ Teal
  Possible in winter.
Top left ~ Yellow
    Flag Iris
Left ~ Mallard
    ducklings

33

ASHTEAD COMMON : Woodland Ramble

DISTANCE : 3 miles approx.

See Information board at START for options to extend the ramble.

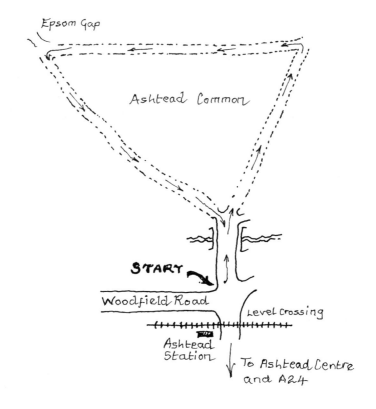

MUD WARNING: Definitely a 'wellies' walk after wet weather and in the winter, or, try it frozen solid!

DOG OWNERS: This is a Site of Special Scientific Interest. If your dog loves to bound off through the undergrowth avoid this site between early spring and autumn or else your dog will disturb some of the rarer ground-nesting birds.

WHEELS: In dry weather the energetic will manage pushchairs but not at all suitable for wheelchairs.

34

ASHTEAD COMMON is not only beautiful woodland flung over a ridge of higher ground but is also of historic importance and one rich in rare wildlife. It is an example of ancient managed woodland complete with the best collection of Oak pollards in the whole country, many of which are over 300 years old. Since 1991 over 200 hectares have been in the keeping of the Corporation of London and are managed by the local community.

OAK POLLARDS are Oak trees which had their tops cut out above the reach of browsing cattle so that the shoots could grow on to yield a crop of timber - anything from poles to construction timber, depending at which age this renewable resource was harvested. Cropping in rotation meant the habitat went through a succession of changes as light was admitted and then gradually decreased as the trees grew back and this attracts a very wide range of plants and creatures. Practically every single plant had its uses in former times. (For booklets on the use of plants in Surrey write to the publisher's address at the front of this book.)

Ashtead Common is now being managed again so you will find new plantings and freshly pollarded trees as the range of ancient habitats is being restored.

START : Turn off the A24 in the middle of Ashtead's main street and go downhill to the station and over the UNEVEN level crossing. The START is in front of you with a large Corporation of London Information Board. Parking for cars in the adjacent roads.

35

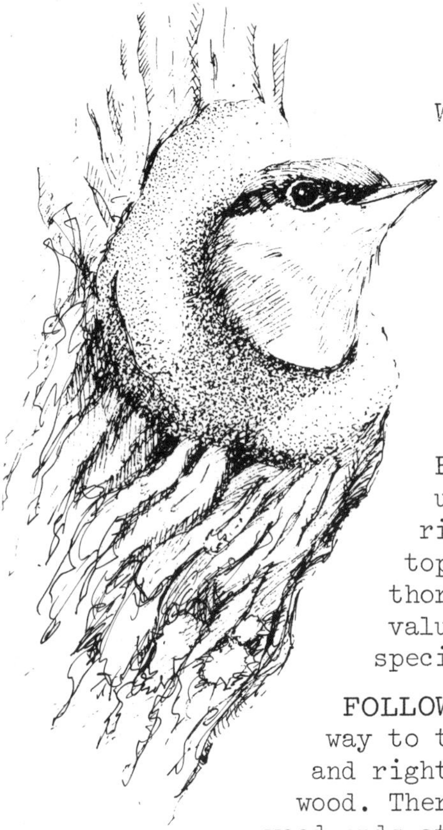

WALK AHEAD along the wide dirt road across the field. This is being managed for meadow flowers and attracts a wide range of 'brown' butterflies.

CROSS THE BRIDGE over the stream. It may now be wet underfoot but if you can cope with this you can manage the rest!

BEAR SLIGHTLY RIGHT to walk up the hillside on the wide grass ride from between the two BLUE-topped marker posts. The thick thorny scrub on either side is very valuable to wildlife; at least 149 species of insect use the Hawthorn.

FOLLOW THE BLUE MARKERS all the way to the crest, down the other side and right through to the far side of the wood. There ARE enough markers. Where the wood ends at the edge of the fields there is another Corporation of London Information Board and also a stout white metal post bearing the arms of the City of London. This is a City of London Coal Duty Boundary Mark, often called a Coal Tax Post. From late medieval times until 1890 the City levied a duty on coal (and wine) crossing the boundary of its jurisdiction, marked by hundreds of these posts, many of which survive. By this means, for example, London was able to finance Sir Christopher Wren's rebuilding scheme after the Great Fire of 1666.

TURN LEFT and follow the track through the woods along the edge of the fields. There are no marker posts along here but they are not needed - just keep to the main track. Look out for another Coal Tax Post and ignore the turning off at this point. Look out also for the good pollards and more open glades that add variety to the habitats. Nuthatches (illustrated above) are among the birds nesting in the tree holes.

36

AT THE END IS THE
EPSOM GAP and another
Information Board to
help you get your
bearings. (If you feel
the need you can leave
here, go out to the
road and there is a
pub just along to the
right!)

TURN LEFT as you
approach the Board,
to cut back into the
woods. At the junction
of paths within sight
BEAR LEFT to take the
route between the WHITE
marker posts. FOLLOW
THE WHITE MARKERS ALL
THE WAY BACK TO THE
START.

. Nightingale .

* * * * * * * * * * * *

SPECIES HIGHLIGHTED ON
THE INFORMATION BOARD:

PURPLE HAIRSTREAK BUTTERFLY

You will do best with binoculars to see this small
butterfly - blackish brown tinged with purplish blue -
as it prefers to fly around the tops of the oaks, in
July and August. Sometimes it comes lower to feed on
the honeydew released by aphids, so keep an eye on
any shrubbery infested with blight.

PURPLE EMPEROR BUTTERFLY

Again binoculars are valuable for finding this insect
for although it is large it too flies around the tops
of the oaks, in July. Only the male has the purple
sheen and then only when angled against the light. In
seeking this you may confuse it with another dark
butterfly with white markings - the White Admiral but

this can be spotted on into August. It has a wonderful swooping flight and more often comes lower, to feed on Bramble nectar.

GRASSHOPPER WARBLERS
These little birds are summer migrants and very hard to see. They can be heard though and once heard are never forgotten because they produce such a lengthy trill. It is likened to an angler's reel being wound in. They nest low down in the grassy scrubby places and are one of the reasons why dogs should be kept under control throughout the nesting season.

NIGHTINGALES
These too are ground or low nesters and resent dog interference. They are also difficult to see, not only for becoming increasingly rare but because they are secretive. Contrary to popular belief they DO sing during the day and even if you have never heard one before you will know this is something special from its volume and sheer quality. Although the Black-cap and Garden Warbler are also fine singers they tend to get breathless whereas the Nightingale phrases its song. Listen a while and it should insert a jug-jug-jug-jug phrase and it can also put a stirring crescendo onto a single note, which no other British bird attempts.

JAY illustrated; important for the way it spreads acorns to keep the woods regenerating.

EWELL VILLAGE : *Village Ramble*

DISTANCE : 1 mile approx.

Route accessible to wheelchairs
     and pushchairs.

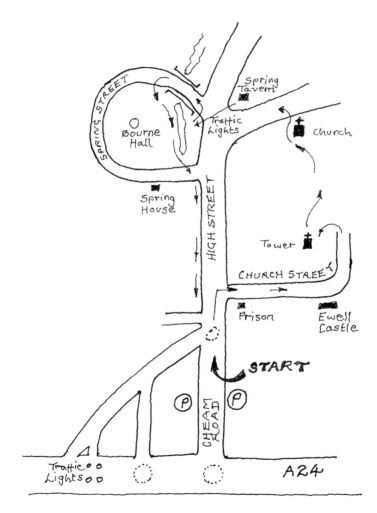

START : one of the CAR PARKS off Cheam Road after
          leaving the A24.

TURN DOWNHILL to head for village centre. Notice the
small shops surviving to create a traditional street
scene, so often destroyed elsewhere by modern rebuilding.

TURN RIGHT into Church Street. Immediately on the
right is the old village lock-up from when Ewell was
responsible for maintaining its own law and order,
hence the barred windows. This is the best survivor of
its type in the county, (see illustration).

The narrow street has an 18th century appearance. Note
Nos. 2 and 4 on the right (both have had their height
increased) and for contrast, the smart roughcast
Warwick Cottage on the left.

The church of St.Michael is set back attractively for
this was once part of the malting site. The Maltsters
comes next, No.6, with the light rippling back from the
hand-made glass of the old windows. This wide frontage
is only a facade to modernise the older timber-framed
building behind, dating from c.1650.

Then comes No.10A, Well House, of c.1700 with six bays
and double doorways under a single porch supported on
Tuscan columns. The pavement is now bordered by a
garden wall - something of note in the Epsom area
where some carry preservation orders. Behind stands
Glyn House with its little tower heralding the rise of
Victorian architecture. This was built in 1839, soon
after the Regency extravaganza that comes next up the
street. This is Ewell Castle, massive and battlemented
and built 1810-14.

BEAR ROUND TO THE LEFT skirting the churchyard.
The medieval church has been destroyed except for the
tower. This was built at the end of the Middle Ages in
the Perpendicular style, which gave England so many
fine church towers. Surrey, alas, has very few of them
and this is the largest. Note the attempts at flint
chequerwork that is such a feature of East Anglian
church architecture. Stoke-next-Guildford has the best
Surrey example of this.

40

The spring Hotel
Ewell.

41

The Old Tower, Ewell

ENTER CHURCHYARD to view the tower. There are also some fine trees of note for the specialist. Find, at the lower northern side of the churchyard, the new (1848) parish church of St.Mary, which was built in a traditional manner. It houses treasures from the old church, including the medieval font, screen (restored) with its rare (in Surrey) dragon head carvings, and the memorial brasses, including the inscription to Edmond Dows "gentilmaoon of the Clerk' of the signett with kyng harry the vii" (siq). The grandest monument is to Sir William Lewen who was Lord Mayor of London in 1717. It is one of Surrey's finer monumental sculptures.

LEAVE the churchyard by the western lychgate, TURN LEFT, CROSS ROAD towards the Spring Tavern with its white weatherboarding which was a popular building style through this part of Surrey.

TURN RIGHT AT THE LIGHTS AND CROSS OVER to enjoy the lakeside of Bourne Hall through the gateway. Beyond the waterside rise the trees and shrubs of the park and above those the unexpected shape of Bourne Hall itself, looking from here like a pinnacled flying saucer, when the leaves are off the trees. It was completed in 1970 (replacing the original Georgian Hall which was a regrettable loss) and is one of the county's more notable buildings of that date.

RETURN TO PAVEMENT and BEAR LEFT on to the bridge with the water either side. There is a waterside walk downstream to the mill for those wishing to extend the ramble. The water comes from a number of underground streams which break the surface hereabouts but not in very dry summers when this beautiful village feature can dry up. All being well, there should be water and reflections, mallard, geese, coot and moorhens. Look out for grey wagtails and kingfishers too, which nest hereabouts.

43

TURN LEFT after the bridge and ENTER THE PARK
Take the lower options to follow paths along the water
side. Look out for black and white tufted ducks. In
the summer the gardens may lure you to explore further.
Try the Bourne Hall to see if exhibitions/museum are of
interest to you on the day of visiting.

TURN LEFT at the top of the water and LEAVE
the Park by the grand gateway.

TURN RIGHT to follow the street back up to the car
park and the starting point, but, architectural
enthusiasts may like to turn hard right at the gateway
to walk along Spring Street to Spring House, a little
way on the left, because it is faced with 'mathematical
tiles' to look like bricks. Look up at the weathered
top to see this rarity clearly.

Bourne Hall

The Upper Mill, Ewell

46

NONSUCH and CHEAM

Parkland
Public Gardens
Architecture

DISTANCE : Over 3 miles with many options to extend.

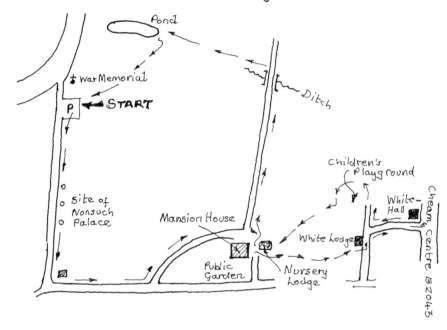

NONSUCH was the fourteenth and last of Henry VIII's London palaces, begun in 1538 with the aim of outshining all other European palaces - there was to be none such like it. Alas in 1682 it was demolished to pay off the gambling debts of Barbara Villiers, Countess of Castlemaine, mistress of Charles II. Today the great Park remains as a public open space, beautiful with trees and grassland, through which it is possible to walk over to Cheam.

WHEELS : Both pushchairs and wheelchairs can follow this route - as far as Cheam but should then return to the Park as the return route listed can be wet and muddy and the grassland will be hard work for wheelchairs.

47

FINDING THE START - From Epsom, follow the A24 for London, through the traffic lights on the Ewell By-pass and at the next set of lights TURN RIGHT (still signed for London). Very soon the road bends to the left and the cross of a war memorial is visible. TURN RIGHT here into the car park.

CHECK closing time of car park on information board.

START from the car park along the surfaced pathway that cuts off along the edge of the park, away from the road. Head for the far end and note en route the ancient Horse Chestnut trees and, on the left, the three obelisks marking the site of the palace. The first marker has a plan and information plate set into it.

TURN LEFT at the far end to continue along the surfaced path through the avenue of trees, with more wide views out over the park.

TAKE FIRST LEFT, another surfaced path, to head off towards the Mansion House. Try a February ramble to see the Snowdrops under the trees behind the Mansion House.

Nonsuch Mansion House

48

GATEWAY TO THE MANSION HOUSE. NONSUCH PARK

Approaching the Mansion House there is, on the right, the entrance to the gardens (NO dogs allowed) and these are well worth a visit, whether at Wisteria time, rose-time or winter to enjoy the trees and evergreens in their landscaped setting. The Nonsuch tree collection is one of the more notable in Surrey. Make your way round anti-clockwise to the exit gatehouse in the wall. (Toilets here). Dog owners continue clockwise round the Mansion House to the gatehouse.

The Mansion House was built 1802-6, by Sir Jeffry Wyatville, in typical Regency style. Note similarities between this and Ewell Castle in the Ewell Village ramble. The latter was built only four years later.

Beside the gatehouse is Nursery Lodge and the option of
walking round the outside wall to view the peacocks etc.
in the aviary (signposted). From outside the aviary the
edge of Cheam can be glimpsed between the trees on the
far side of the grassland.

HEAD ACROSS THE GRASS towards the distant car park
but skirt left of it and cut out across the park, through
the strip of woodland and on over the grass again. A
white lodge will come into view - head for that. For
wheels, instead of cutting across the grass proceed from
the gatehouse along the surfaced path, turn left at the
end and at the exit take the pavement round to the white
lodge.

**EXIT at the WHITE LODGE. TURN LEFT and FIRST
RIGHT into PARK LANE**

The modern buildings at the start of Park Lane soon give
way to very attractive 17th/18th century cottages, white
weatherboarded, following the curve and then nudging
each other up the
short hill.

Park
Lane

Whitehall, Cheam

At the top of Park Lane, on the left, is Whitehall - a
15th century timber-framed house with 16th century and
Georgian additions and alterations. For a small admiss-
ion fee you can wander upstairs and downstairs and all
around inside. There are various exhibits and very clear
explanations in each room of the evolution of that part
of the building, with significant features left exposed
to view. There is nowhere else quite like this in Surrey
and the quality of exposition would be difficult to
better anywhere. Whitehall is well worth a visit. Check
opening hours. Refreshments available.

Whitehall also has tourist information for the Borough
and a map showing where the other interesting buildings
are situated in Cheam. Therefore this ramble can be
easily extended to take in more of Cheam. As you leave
Whitehall it is worth turning left to view its old
neighbouring buildings and the Georgian Rectory. The
church opposite dates from 1862-4 (better from the outside as a piece of townscaping than from the inside).
The remains of the medieval church constitute the
Lumley Chapel in the churchyard.

RETRACE ROUTE DOWN PARK LANE and **TURN RIGHT** at the bottom.
Wheels – return to Park and choose own route back; the following route can be wet and muddy after rain.

ENTER RECREATION GROUND
FOLLOW FENCE ROUND THE
CHILDREN'S PLAY AREA.

FOLLOW FENCE UP
SIDE OF PLAYING
FIELDS TO LEAVE
BY GATE AT TOP
LEFT CORNER
INTO THE
WOODS.

FOLLOW
TRACK
DOWN
THROUGH
TREES.

The Nursery
Lodge comes
into view and a
route can be taken
across the park to the
car park....or...

THE BROADWAY, CHEAM

SKIRT MANSION HOUSE ANTI-CLOCKWISE AND TURN
OFF RIGHT TO FOLLOW SURFACED PATH OUT INTO THE
PARK.

TURN LEFT when the path crosses a ditch.

FOLLOW DITCH DOWN THE GRASSLAND TO THE POND.
This route can be wet underfoot, especially in the winter.
The pond was dug a few years ago to help drain this part
of the park. It's attractive in summer with waterlilies.
BEWARE – the car park ahead is not the starting point!

CROSS THE DITCH JUST ABOVE THE POND and proceed
ahead. A fenced picnic area comes into view towards the
right and beyond that is the car park and starting point.

BANSTEAD WOODS : Downland and Ancient Woodland

DISTANCE : 3 miles approx.
Options for extending

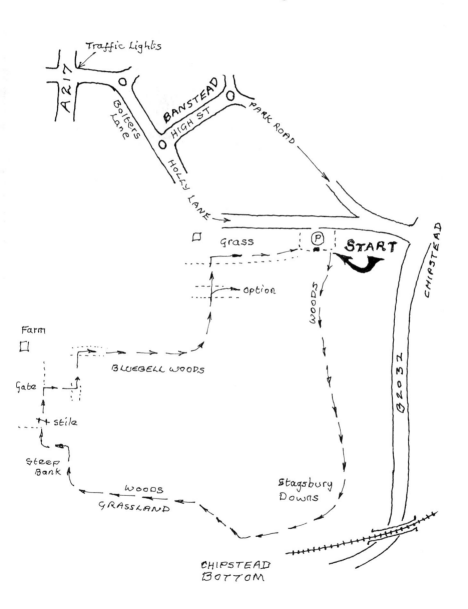

BANSTEAD VILLAGE lies off to the south east of Epsom and can be reached easily by road. Head for the village centre to pick up the directions listed at the head of the ramble route.

Banstead is convenient for getting refreshment but is otherwise a rather disappointing place. It has been rebuilt almost completely this century and not with the finest architecture. For some, this will be a good reason to stop but for anyone seeking old village charm there is little reward. The old well at the end of Park Road attracts visitors and the medieval church has remarkably survived. It looks Victorian from the outside (work of G.E.Street, 1861; see Headley notes) but the interior has much of interest, going back to the late 12th century. Banstead used to be a much more important place than it is today. A summer visit is the more rewarding when containers of flowers etc. improve the scene.

BANSTEAD HIGH STREET

Red Admiral

BANSTEAD WOODS, like Ashtead Common in this book, is known to scientists and conservationists as Ancient Woodland. It is not simply old but has special wildlife associations which are found only on such sites. Here also, the site includes areas of chalk downland pasture, rich in the special flora of the chalk.

The site (250 acres) is administered by Reigate and Banstead Borough Council who permit public access except to areas undergoing conservation schemes. In particular, sheep grazing has been re-introduced in special fenced areas to reduce scrub encroachment and encourage the special downland turf, with its specific wild flowers, butterflies etc. The Red Admiral and the Comma butterflies illustrated here are not particularly special to these downland habitats but look out for some of the blue species.

Many rewarding hours can be spent throughout the year getting to know this site and then the adjoining areas and footpaths. Out of all these options just one route which is easy to follow , has been chosen as an introduction.

LOCATION: From Banstead - turn left at the bottom of the High Street and follow that road (Holly Lane, B2219) to the car park (about 1.3 mls) or, from the top of the High Street turn right and follow Park Road to the end, turn right, and car park is on the left (about 1.5 miles). Grid ref. TQ 274583.

Comma

PARKING : off-road car park, with toilets, provided.

START: Through the gate in the top left corner of the car park (to the left of the toilets). Follow the main path up the hillside towards the woodland and bear left with the path to go along the side of the wood rather than be tempted to take one of the paths into it.

FOLLOW this route all along the top of the Downs beside the wood, with views into the Chipstead Valley below or across to further rounded downland scenery beyond. This is real chalk country, with massive Beech trees, broody dark Yews, red-stemmed Dogwoods and aromatic herbs. The route changes all the while, sometimes through trees, sometimes through scrub and at other times more grassy.

CONTINUE out into the fields and very soon a cross-track is reached which can be ignored. Carry on ahead, following the line of the valley, even though the path becomes narrower. Very soon the path divides left and right of a hedge and here take the RIGHT fork (but the left one rejoins it if you prefer). There are good views all along here including a sighting of a railway viaduct down in the valley; the local railway history is quite interesting to the enthusiast.

The route reaches the end of the chalk ridge which swings round to the right as Stagsbury Downs with Chipstead Bottom below. Here is one of the sites where sheep have been re-introduced for reclamation purposes. Should the fencing still be there when you arrive follow it down to the Bottom. If it has gone

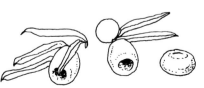

Yew berries (toxic)

White Campion

do not bear off
to the right but continue
on the same track over the
lip of the Downs and so towards
the Bottom and the railway line.
The path swings to the right and
cuts through thick scrub and woodland:
a very different habitat and another
range of wildlife.

At the end of the woody section ignore
the left fork but on emerging on to
the grassland **FORK RIGHT** to take
the path up across the grassland to
the edge of the main wood and then to
follow it right along to the far end.
This stretch is thick with beautiful
yellow Rock Roses in summer, plus many
other species of the chalk flora.

BEAR RIGHT at the end to follow the route
up the steep bank, over the tree roots, as it
follows the end of the woodland.

TURN LEFT at the top to follow the grassy ride.
This is one of many areas devastated by the hurricane
in 1987 and demonstrates the speed and density with
which the open beechwood floor has regenerated. About
a third of the ancient trees here were lost at that
time. Now as the fallen trees rot away they provide a
valuable habitat for fungi and invertebrates. Do not
break open the rotten wood to see, as that destroys
the very habitat that interests you.

CROSS THE STILE into the pasture and heed the notice
to follow the path along the side of the wood.

TURN RIGHT at the first gateway into the wood and
proceed ahead.

TURN LEFT at the trackway. Note the foreign Larch
trees, adding more variety to the wood and attracting
their own special birds to feed on the ripening seed
in the cones.

TURN RIGHT at the T-junction and follow the broad
ride all the way through the wood. This is always a
beautiful walk but especially so when the Bluebells not
only add rich colour to the woodland floor but fill the
air with scent. Keep to the ride - trampling on the
Bluebell leaves weakens their bulbs.

Eventually this ride reaches a T-junction with another
broad ride at the far side of the wood and here there
is a choice. Dog owners are recommended to TURN RIGHT
and follow the route back to the car park. This avoids
disturbing ponies in the field ahead. Otherwise, cross
the ride and continue ahead to the edge of the field to
go through the kissing gate
and then   TURN RIGHT to
follow along the
edge of the wood
to the car park.

THE WELL - PARK ROAD - BANSTEAD

HEADLEY HEATH : Heathland and Downland.

DISTANCE : 3½ miles approx.

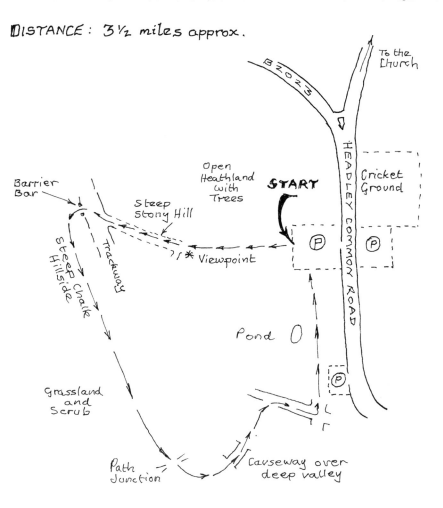

WHEELS : Not suitable.
         Pushchairs possible around car park area.

HEADLEY HEATH (Headley Common) lies over the hills to the south, in an area where there are many fine walks. This particular site, part on sandstone, part on chalk, is of special scientific value and is administered by The National Trust accordingly.

This ramble is divided into two to cater for all tastes. Firstly there is the option of wandering around the church area. Secondly, a route out over the countryside is described.

THE CHURCH AREA

Headley is a scattering of cottages and church over the hill, with no obvious centre, although the church spire is a landmark for miles around. The old cottages and farms reveal themselves gradually as the rambler explores the local area.

Inside the churchyard gate there is a weird domed building. It contains a blocked medieval window, a slate decalogue and the memorial to Elizabeth and Ferdinand Faithful. He was a former incumbent. Their daughter Emily became publisher and printer to Queen Victoria. This was all created from materials taken from the medieval church when it was rebuilt.

The site of the old church is marked out with clipped Yew trees in the churchyard. The flints from that church were re-used by G.E.Street for building the tower of the present church, in 1859. They have been knapped and set to create a hard black and grey surface. In contrast, when Anthony Salvin built the chancel in 1855 he used flints taken from the local fields and when knapped set them to reveal the beautiful russett staining through their interiors. For the nave he used whole flints set proud. What a range of effects from the same material!

This is the only example of Salvin's work in Surrey. He rarely accepted church commissions anywhere.

Don't miss the sundial over the south door; another rarity in Surrey.

THE RAMBLE has been chosen from those recommended for being easy to follow and for taking in both the sandstone and the chalk habitats. It does cover some steepish ups and downs which may not suit ramblers with hip problems. There is however plenty of scope to explore the more level heathland that adjoins the car park. In all there are 530 acres in the care of The National Trust.

Ling

CAR PARKING : Either side of Headley Common Road, adjacent to the cricket green, (follow lane south from the church). This site can be very popular at peak recreation times but there is another car park a little further south, on the right. There is a CHARGE FOR CAR PARKING.

START in the main car park, turning your back to the road and leaving through the centre of the rear bank. Take the most worn route straight ahead.

CONTINUE AHEAD down over the heathland, heading away from the car park. The scenery is typical of heathland with grass and bracken, birch and heather. The three species of heather are illustrated. The route drops down along a stony section and then out over the grass again. By this time there is a grand sense of wide open space and the "short walk visitors" are being left behind. When the route becomes less distinct aim for the brink of the land ahead. It is a viewpoint with seating, looking out over the hills and valleys. People with push-chairs are recommended to turn back here.

CONTINUE AHEAD down the steep stony track to the junction of routes in the valley below. The geology has now changed from sandstone to chalk and flint so there is a complete change of flora. The chalk flora on the right hand bank is worth a close look in its

season. Remember, it is against the law to pick the flowers.

CROSS THE BOTTOM TRACK TO GO UNDER THE CROSS-BAR AND TAKE THE ROUTE OFF TO THE LEFT

This swings back left to climb the steep chalk hillside on this flank of the hillside. Again there are wonderful chalkland flowers such as the aromatic Marjoram and the Thymes. There are also some seats which you may well appreciate. Be sure to turn round for the views behind.

CONTINUE AHEAD when the hill levels off. Follow the same main track, keeping to the left side to avoid being lured off along other tempting routes. You may well find sheep enclosures somewhere along the route where the National Trust have reintroduced traditional grazing. This is to reduce the scrub that is invading the special chalk grassland. It should also encourage the chalkland flowers which have adapted to sheep – grazed land over the last couple of thousand years and more. Dog owners are of course requested to keep their pets under strict control whenever in the proximity of the sheep.

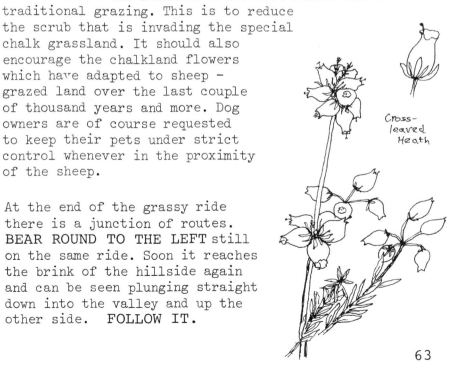

Cross-leaved Heath

At the end of the grassy ride there is a junction of routes. **BEAR ROUND TO THE LEFT** still on the same ride. Soon it reaches the brink of the hillside again and can be seen plunging straight down into the valley and up the other side. **FOLLOW IT.**

63

The track crosses the valley bottom by a causeway, as it is wet and has a pool, all attracting a different range of wildlife.

BEAR SLIGHTLY RIGHT at the junction of the routes at the top of the hill, to continue along the same track. It may well have wheel marks left by the maintenance vehicles.

TURN RIGHT when it meets a main unsurfaced roadway and follow it to the end. This can get a covering of mud in winter but it is not deep and there are little side paths to avoid it if preferred.

TURN LEFT at the end to follow another track back to the main car park. This route will pass a little pond for additional variety. If you have parked in the second smaller car park further south down Headley Common Road you will pass within sight of it by continuing to follow these directions. You can then turn right to cut back to your car.

LYCH GATE AT REAR OF HEADLEY CHURCH
WITH VIEW OF EPSOM DOWNS